Thimbles
and Thimble Cases

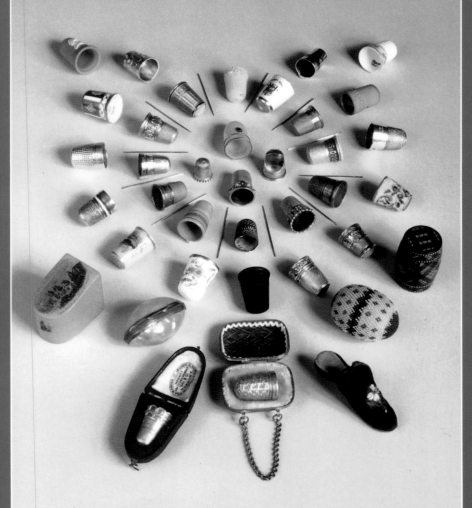

Eleanor Johnson

A Shire Book

The Shire Book

Thimbles
and Thimble Cases

Eleanor Johnson

A collection of thimbles. Showing great variety in their materials, design and decoration, they make a fascinating subject for collectors.

Published in 2003 by Shire Publications Ltd,
Cromwell House, Church Street, Princes Risborough,
Buckinghamshire HP27 9AA, UK.
(Website: www.shirebooks.co.uk)

British Library Cataloguing in Publication Data:
Johnson, Eleanor
Thimbles and Thimble Cases. – 2nd ed.
1. Thimbles 2. Thimbles – History
3. Thimbles – Collectors and collecting
I. Title 646.1'9
ISBN 0 7478 0403 6

Cover: *A display of thimbles and thimble cases.*

ACKNOWLEDGEMENTS

The author gratefully acknowledges the loan of thimbles and thimble cases for the photo
graphs from Audrey, Elaine, Jean, the two Joans, Sylvia and Kay Havemann-Mart. She
would also like to acknowledge most gratefully her debt to her husband, Alan, for supplying
much of the necessary information. She also thanks the following for the provision o
photographs: Crummles & Company, of Poole, page 26 (top); the late George Mell, page 18
(all); Old Hall Tableware, of Bloxwich, page 26 (centre); Royal Worcester Spode, pages 26
(bottom), 27 (top); the Wedgwood Group, page 27 (bottom). Other photography is acknowl
edged as follows: Michael Bass, pages 1, 7 (all), 11 (bottom), 14 (both), 15 (all), 19, 31, 34
(both), 35 (both), 38; David A. Ross LRPS, pages 3, 4, 6, 8, 9 (both), 10, 11 (top), 12 (both), 13
(both), 16, 17 (both), 20 (both), 21 (both), 22 (both), 23, 24 (both), 25 (both), 28 (all), 29 (all), 30
32 (all), 33 (both), 36 (both), 37 (both), 39, 40 (both) and cover.

A SPECIAL ACKNOWLEDGEMENT

The author would like to acknowledge the special debt owed by collectors and others
interested in thimbles to Mr Edwin Holmes, whose untimely death occurred in 1997, for his
long-standing research and matchless knowledge, recorded in his two irreplaceable books
Thimbles (1976) and *A History of Thimbles* (1985).

Printed in Great Britain by CIT Printing Services Ltd,
Press Buildings, Merlins Bridge, Haverfordwest,
Pembrokeshire SA61 1XF.

Contents

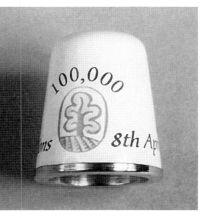

An enamelled thimble commissioned in 1997 to cel-
ebrate the sale of 100,000 copies of the Shire Album
'Thimbles' by Eleanor Johnson, the predecessor of this
book. Only two such thimbles were made.

Silver thimbles with the names of towns, made by Henry Griffiths & Sons of Leamington Spa and a[l]
hallmarked, with the brand name THE SPA, except for the one named Combe Martin, which is marke[d]
STERLING SILVER, THE SPA, MADE IN ENGLAND. (Top row, left to right) Minehead; Croydon; St Leonards[:]
Combe Martin. (Centre row, left to right) Birmingham; Reading; Stratford; Southsea; Edinburgh[:]
(Centre front) Scarborough.

Collecting thimbles

The wide variety of thimbles that have been made surprises man[y]
people, who regard a thimble merely as a basic tool for sewing, made i[n]
a single shape, in a limited number of styles and patterns and in a smal[l]
range of materials. By definition a thimble is a cap worn to protect th[e]
finger while pushing a needle through cloth. It is shaped somewha[t]
like a bell, sometimes open-topped, and usually worn on the middl[e]
finger of the hand. The origin of the word is the old English *thymel*
'thumb stall', and in Germany the very apt name is *Fingerhut*, literall[y]
'finger hat'. Nowadays a thimble is a widely used aid to sewing, know[n]
throughout the world in various forms, and thimbles have for man[y]
years been among the most popularly collected objects, possibly o[n]
account of their wide variety and their small size, which makes the[m]
easy to display in a small space. They are made in a wide range o[f]
materials, sizes and shapes, and the diversity of their decoration give[s]
them an indefinable charm, from the smallest sizes made for childre[n]
through a number of utilitarian types to those of a more luxurious kind[.]
Many quite humble types have interest, as they set us wondering abou[t]

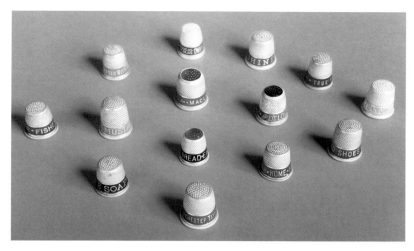

Aluminium advertising thimbles. Three have coloured glass tops. The products and services featured on the coloured bands are: (left to right, and moving down the vertical rows from top to bottom) FISHER THE JEWELLER; YOU CAN COOK BETTER WITH GAS; COLMAN'S MUSTARD; OLD HOME SOAP; FOR COUGHS AND COLDS, OWBRIDGE'S LUNG TONIC; MACLEOD'S DALMASCO TEA *(with red glass top);* EASY THREAD *(with red glass top);* TAYLOR'S LAUNDRY, DORCHESTER; SUNSHINE; USE DR LOVELACE'S SOAP *(with green glass top);* HOOVER HOME HAPPINESS; TRUE FIT BOOT SHOP; WOOD'S GOOD SHOES; HANCOCK'S MUTUAL LIFE INSURANCE, BOSTON.

Workaday thimbles

Four very desirable vegetable ivory thimbles with matching thimble holders, in different carved designs. Vegetable ivory is the corozo nut, the very large kernel of a palm.

Although most collectors are mainly interested in the more unusual and decorative examples of thimbles, some of the everyday, utilitarian ones, used for household sewing, do have charm and interest. Many were made in base metals, such as steel, brass, cupro-nickel (an alloy of copper and nickel), nickel silver and aluminium. In addition bone and early plastics (one of which was known as Xylonite) were used. One fairly common thimble of this type, in cream-coloured plastic and marked in some cases 'Halex', resembles ivory at first glance, but a closer inspection and greater familiarity will enable the collector to distinguish between the two. The plastic material seems lighter and less dense. The collector should be wary of being offered the plastic examples for ivory (see the next chapter). Ivory was always a costly material, and on a larger object the silky, wavy grain should be seen, but this might be difficult on a thimble. Bone thimbles are rare, and the material has a generally coarser appearance than ivory, though a similar colour, and may have small dark vertical streaks on the surface, which are quite distinctive. Coloured plastics are common for thimbles, but one

rather less common type is shaped like the tip of a thumb with its nail.

There is a wide variety of metal thimbles, perhaps the commonest being steel; some of these are plain steel, but others are lined with brass, the rolled-back lower rim giving the first indication of this type. They are susceptible to rusting. The only decoration is the usual indentations all over. Brass thimbles are often similarly plain, or they may have a variety of attractive and interesting

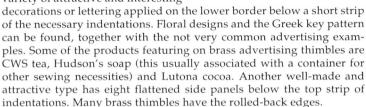

decorations or lettering applied on the lower border below a short strip of the necessary indentations. Floral designs and the Greek key pattern can be found, together with the not very common advertising examples. Some of the products featuring on brass advertising thimbles are CWS tea, Hudson's soap (this usually associated with a container for other sewing necessities) and Lutona cocoa. Another well-made and attractive type has eight flattened side panels below the top strip of indentations. Many brass thimbles have the rolled-back edges.

Among the most practical thimbles, popular with many collectors, are those with the proprietary names Dorcas, Doris, Dreema and Dura. These thimbles have a thin layer of steel sandwiched between two layers of silver. Silver is a soft metal, and so this type is more durable than solid silver. Some are fairly plain with indentations, while others have more interesting decoration.

Aluminium advertising thimbles are another utilitarian group. They are very light in weight and have a coloured band around the base on which is printed the name of the product; some have an inset glass top. The most common colours are red, green and blue, but less frequently yellow will be found. Unfortunately the colours are often badly worn, and the most desirable thimbles are those in which the colour is in good condition. Numerous products were advertised in this way, and some examples are illustrated on page 9. A similar type that has been seen is 'Frae bonnie Scotland'. Advertising thimbles also come from the United States, but these will be described in the chapter on 'Worldwide thimbles'.

Old examples of wooden thimbles are now rare, but many such originated in Austria and Germany. Their shapes are usually fairly simple, indented or with concentric turned rings, and they are made in boxwood, fruitwoods, rosewood and occasionally in bog-oak, a petrified wood from Irish peat bogs. Bog-oak thimbles were probably made as souvenirs from Killarney or other parts of Ireland and sometimes bear a shamrock motif.

Wooden thimbles, with a skein of Filoselle thread. (Left to right) Large bog-oak thimble with domed top; turned rosewood with concentric rings; turned fruitwood with concentric rings; a quite rare light-coloured early Tunbridge ware example with concentric rings painted in green, black and red; carved bog-oak with a shamrock design.

A group of steel-topped silver thimbles – a very practical type. Silver, being a soft metal, goes into holes as a result of constant use of a needle. Four of these thimbles have a band of indentations in the upper part of the sides; the plain part has varied decorations, and the thimble on the far left has a beaded lower rim. Two others have rolled-back edges.

Thimbles for the accomplished needlewoman

Towards the end of the eighteenth century artistic needlework became a popular pastime in fashionable circles, and it continued to be throughout the nineteenth century. As middle and upper class ladies sat at home awaiting callers, they occupied themselves with fine embroidery, as well as with other crafts. Fine cambric handkerchiefs, tiny patchwork pincushions, needlecases, watch pockets, hair-tidies and every conceivable useful article were made. Fine petit point embroidery was popular, and later the coarser, brightly coloured Berlin wool tapestry work. Long visits to relatives and friends were commonplace, as described by Jane Austen in her novels. Most wealthy people indulged in frequent social gatherings in the evenings, during the season in Bath, London or other fashionable centres, or during the rest of the year at home in town or the country. At these social occasions, while some members of the party might play cards or sit and join in conversation, it was perfectly permissible for other ladies to occupy themselves with their needlework. The items on which they were working provided topics for conversation and subjects for comment and admiration.

For these ladies a silver thimble was a welcome gift. Before the late nineteenth century, when the duty was withdrawn, English thimbles bore no hallmark as this was not required by law for items under 5 pennyweights (approximately 14 grams). The duty had been high, making hallmarked articles more expensive than the silver coinage, in order to prevent coins from being melted down. The hallmark, when applied, consists of the emblem of a lion, to denote that the article is silver, a symbol for the assay office, a letter to give the date, and often the maker's initials. Some makers are well known, for instance Henry Griffiths of

A hallmarked English silver thimble, with the maker's initials, HG & S (Henry Griffiths & Son), the anchor for Birmingham Assay Office, the lion denoting 92.5 per cent purity of silver, the date letter F for 1930 and the size 15. This souvenir from Minehead has a daisy design on the upper part.

11

Commemorative thimbles of brass and silver. (Top row, left to right) Brass, THE BRITISH EMPIRE EXHIBITION; silver, with scenic border, for the Kensington Exhibition, 1862; a purple plastic box with the date 1910, a red crown and the date 1935, the initials G and M, and underneath SILVER JUBILEE, containing a silver thimble also commemorating the Silver Jubilee of King George V and Queen Mary, the hallmark having the heads of both the King and the Queen, and the word SILVER on the rim; brass, THE BRITISH EMPIRE EXHIBITION; silver with black enamel on white, for the Investiture of Prince Charles at Caernarvon Castle in 1969. (Centre row, left to right) Silver with red, white and blue enamel bands and the message A STITCH FOR THE RED WHITE AND BLUE; silver for the Great Exhibition of 1851; enamel on silver, for the Jubilee of Queen Elizabeth II, with her portrait; silver, for the same Jubilee; brass, for the Silver Jubilee of King George V and Queen Mary. (Bottom row, left to right) Nickel, for the coronation of King George V and Queen Mary; silver for Queen Victoria's Diamond Jubilee; enamel on silver, for the Winston Churchill centenary 1874-1974; silver, Brighton Pavilion; silver, for the wedding of Queen Victoria and Prince Albert.

A collection of English silver thimbles, showing a wide variety of the designs and types of indentations to be found. In the centre, in its original case with the name of the retailing jeweller on white silk inside the lid, is a thimble known as 'Cable'; a similar one is just below and to the right of it. A thimble of this design was said to have been used to improvise a battery to enable the cable of the Atlantic Telegraph to be tested. The actual thimble was later presented to the British Museum, where it was displayed.

Silver thimbles with semi-precious stones. (Top row of four thimbles, left to right) Thimble with alternating green and turquoise stones set in the lower border; similar, with turquoise and pearls alternating; coral stones with applied decoration; green stones with gilt applied decoration. (Bottom row from far left) Amethyst stone top with indentations and chevron-engraved lower border; amethyst with indentations and applied silver decorated lower border; plain with engraved swags and cornelian top; moonstone top; Connemara marble with shamrock-decorated border, marked J S & S, DUBLIN, 1933; dark green stone top.

Enamel thimbles. (Top row, left to right) Silver with white enamel featuring a squirrel on a branch; Norwegian silver with a moonstone top and royal blue guilloche enamel; Norwegian silver with a moonstone top and pale green guilloche enamel, 1900; Norwegian silver with moonstone top and Scandinavian snow scene with dog sledge, 1900; Norwegian silver with a gilded top and polar bears in Arctic setting, 1930s; white enamel on brass with a black design; brass with white enamel and a blue floral design, 1960. (Centre row) Plain Norwegian silver with blue enamel triangles over a white spotted lower ring, 1910; silver with a deep purple lower band; silver with plain reeded sides and a dark green top; silver with dark blue enamel sides featuring a squirrel against a yellow oval; Staffordshire enamel on brass, royal blue with a gold fleur-de-lis design; Crummles of Poole, white enamel with a red, yellow and blue design, similar to the one above in plain white and black. (Bottom three) White enamel on brass, commemorating the Silver Jubilee of Queen Elizabeth II; silver with a rose garland on a white band; Norwegian silver with a moonstone top and a design of black sailing boats on a fjord, 1900.

A collection of enamel thimbles, one old one with a copper top and the inscription A GIFT OF LOVE, but mainly modern and from several countries: having floral decoration, a delicate butterfly, windmills, one with a moonstone top and blue and white spots, and another commemorating the Royal Wedding of Prince Charles and Lady Diana Spencer in 1981.

Leamington Spa (usually with the Birmingham hallmark) and Charles Horner of Halifax (with the Chester hallmark). Items made by these firms are much sought after by collectors, but there are others who are less well known.

Among the wide variety of silver thimbles are some commemorative ones, now very scarce. The Silver Jubilee of King George V and Queen Mary was marked in this way, and the hallmarks for the years 1934 and 1935 have their heads added alongside. The coronation of Elizabeth II was similarly marked with the addition of her head for the years 1952 and 1953.

Silver thimbles come in a wide variety, and many are elaborately decorated. Some have pictures around the lower rim, many of these being souvenirs; others have inscriptions or the name of a place, for instance 'Minehead' or 'Isle of Man'. Some of these thimbles have tops made of indented semi-precious stones, such as amethyst, cornelian or moonstone. For the present-day collector, silver thimbles provide the greatest choice, many of the designs being interesting and attractive. Silver advertising thimbles that have been noted include: 'Hovis bread'; 'Andrews liver salts'; 'Conroy Couch, Torquay'; 'Steel and Company,

Seven commemorative thimbles. (Left to right) Silver with a gilt crown and a band of processional figures, for the coronation of King George V and Queen Mary in 1911; silver for Queen Victoria's Diamond Jubilee; a modern silver thimble with the inscription MOLLY PITCHER, MONMOUTH 1976; two silver metal thimbles inscribed VICTORIA JUBILEE; silver for the coronation of Elizabeth II in 1953 showing the Queen's head in the hallmark; and a silver-plated thimble for the coronation of Edward VII and Queen Alexandra in 1902.

A mixed group of silver thimbles, one with an amethyst top, and showing some typical types of ornamentation.

er thimbles with inscriptions, in-
ing FORGET-ME-NOT *and* THE LA-
FRIEND. Place-names include ISLE
MAN, FELIXSTOWE *(with a cornelian*
, LLANDUDNO and MINEHEAD. *Ad-*
ising examples include VINCENT'S
YEOVIL, HOVIS, CONROY COUCH,
QUAY, ANDREWS LIVER SALTS, JAMES
KER THE LONDON JEWELLER *and*
S WALKER WISHES YOU LUCK; this
was given to a couple when they
hased a wedding ring. One further
ller's item (shown open end up)
the inscription applied in the re-
e manner to normal.

Whitley Bay'; and 'Vincents of Yeovil'. Some bear the inscription 'James Walker, the London jeweller' or 'James Walker wishes you luck'. These were given by the jewellers to the purchasers of wedding rings. Silver thimbles were also made engraved with the names of the ships of the Peninsular and Oriental Steamship Company.

Ivory thimbles, although not now very plentiful, add interest to a collection. Some are quite plain and others decorated, dyed or painted. Many late eighteenth-century and nineteenth-century workboxes contained a thimble matching the other tools inside, which often came from China, and it is these that usually come on to the market today.

Silver thimbles. (Clockwise from far left) An early type with hand-punched indentations; one decorated with gold stars; one with alternating smooth and decorated panels; a thimble shaped like the tip of a finger; another with a decorated band; one with a cartouche on which to engrave initials; one with a band having a design of buildings; and one with a shield also for engraving initials; with a blue velvet-lined egg-shaped silver thimble holder in the centre.

15

Luxury thimbles

More delicate and somewhat impractical thimbles were made, perhaps for a special gift, to be used only occasionally or just as a showpiece. Some of these, for example those made in porcelain, were said to be ideal for sewing delicate fabrics such as silk, because they would be less likely to catch the fine threads. In this category also come thimbles made in mother-of-pearl, tortoiseshell, enamel, gold and silver filigree. Pinchbeck thimbles are also included here because of their present rarity; pinchbeck is an inexpensive substitute for gold made from zinc and copper and named after the inventor, Christopher Pinchbeck.

Mother-of-pearl thimbles are particularly attractive and desirable, though now extremely scarce and expensive. They were made in distinctive shapes, having a more pointed or domed top than is usual. Fine indentations cover the top and part of the sides, and some thimbles have fine gilt metal bands around the bottom and a small oval with a coloured pansy attached to the side. These are known as Palais Royal thimbles after the French district in which they were made.

Another rare and valuable kind of thimble was made in tortoiseshell. These are the usual shape but many have no indentations, so perhaps they were never intended for actual use. They are of very fragile construction and often have gold and silver inlay. One type, now rarely seen, is known as Piercy's Patent.

Ivory, mother-of-pearl and tortoiseshell thimbles. (Back row, left to right) Mother-of-pearl Palais Royal thimble with a small oval shield featuring a pansy; plain mother-of-pearl Palais Royal; tortoiseshell with gold top and inlaid gold decoration on the sides; small ivory thimble with hand-punched indentations and gold rim; ivory with carved lower band. (Three below) Tortoiseshell, with gold lower band; plain ivory with narrow carved lower band; ivory with hand-punched indentations and plain lower band.

Thimbles of gold and of gold with silver. (Top left) Thimble with a gold indented top, the sides plain silver with niello decoration, American. (Centre left) Two gold thimbles with turquoise stones set into the border. (Bottom left) Three-colour gold thimble with an applied gold ring between concentric rings. (Bottom centre) Gold thimble decorated round the lower border with a scene from La Fontaine's 'Fables'. (Top right) Silver with some gold, a Charles Horner original with the Chester hallmark for 1900. (Top centre) Gold thimble with silver and an ivy-leaf design. (Centre far right) Silver thimble with gold decorated lower border and scalloped edge, American. (Bottom right) An example with gold and silver decoration, American. (In the middle) Plain gold thimble with no indentations, an amethyst top and a little delicate engraved decoration, Norwegian.

Fine thimbles of enamel on silver or copper were made, frequently beautifully decorated on the sides; the indentations were on the top only, on a metal plate for extra strength. They were originally made in the early nineteenth century in the Midlands, and subsequently at Battersea in London, but only for a comparatively short period. They are easily damaged, and good condition is all-important in a specimen found, but they are now seldom seen except in museums and an occasional collection. Russian, German, Dutch and Norwegian ones were also made.

Most thimble collectors aim to own at least one gold thimble. They were made in great variety, some being plain apart from the indentations, while others have fine decoration on the sides. The old

A group of now quite rare early nineteenth-century filigree silver thimbles and containers. (Left) A combination example, shown closed, with the thimble screwing on to the base, which contains a tape-measure. (Right) Filigree combination with the thimble removed to show the blue glass scent bottle that fits inside the thimble. (Bottom) A thimble with a plain oval cartouche on which to engrave initials.

17

Left: *A Norwegian enamel on silver thimble with a hardstone top, depicting a sailing boat in mountain scenery.*
Centre: *An unmarked early porcelain thimble, white with painted decoration of buildings, trees, water and a sailing boat. It could be from the Meissen factory.*
Right: *An Italian silver-gilt thimble with finely engraved lower band, inset with coral stones.*

ones seldom bore a hallmark, this not being required by law and the duty being so high, but most twentieth-century examples have a hallmark and a size number. Among the most desirable of gold thimbles are those having precious or semi-precious stones set into the lower part of the sides, but these are now rare and can be expensive. Gold thimbles were also produced in France and the United States, where Simons Brothers were well-known makers.

Filigree silver thimbles, though now scarce and expensive, are very beautiful when in good condition, but by the nature of their construction they are prone to damage. They can be found in a most desirable form as a screw-on cover for a blue or plain glass scent bottle that rests in a small base. Another type has the addition of a tapemeasure. In some of these the thimble part was made in plain silver.

Another expensive and rare type of thimble is made in silver gilt. The gilt easily wore off, and examples in good condition are seldom found.

Many beautiful porcelain thimbles were made, being most popular in the second quarter of the nineteenth century. They have now become comparatively scarce and expensive. Perhaps the best-known were made by the Royal Worcester porcelain factory. They were made over quite a long period and can be dated from the mark (or lack of it) inside the thimble. The porcelain used was very fine and often of the distinctive creamy colour associated with this factory. The decoration, frequently of birds, was hand-painted and signed by the artist. One highly regarded artist, whose work is now much sought after, was William Powell. A hunchback and a delightful character, he had a deep love for his bird subjects, which he so keenly observed and sensitively portrayed. Some other porcelain manufacturers also made thimbles, notably Meissen of Germany and Coalport and Derby in England. Meissen thimbles are extremely rare outside museums and collections, and far too costly for most collectors. Other English porcelain examples are found occasionally, but these tend to be expensive.

Novelties and oddities

In the early days thimbles for general use were made only in a very few basic sizes, but as time went on the range was much enlarged. Collectors of thimbles often feel that former sizes seem impractically small. Many nineteenth-century thimbles are of normal size, but it may be that the fingers of some of our ancestors were more slender, especially if their hands were not accustomed to rough work. However, amongst the most delightful finds for the collector are the small thimbles made for children. Single examples are quite plentiful, although a complete set, usually comprising three in gradually increasing sizes, is now seldom found. Little girls were taught to sew when very young, the samplers they so painstakingly completed bearing witness to their labours. But the lesson was essential, for women had to be able to make the family garments and household necessities, unless they could afford a daily sewing woman, and sewing machines did not become readily available until towards the end of the nineteenth century.

Thimbles from different parts of the world, photographed with a beautifully made ivory basket thimble holder, probably of eastern origin. (Top row, left to right) A nickel thimble with a magnetic top, probably German; a continental silver type with a hardstone top; a modern Mexican silver example with applied decoration; one in Russian silver. (Middle row, left to right) A continental silver type with a hardstone top and applied shield; a similar all-silver thimble with a shield and plain band decoration; another continental silver one with hardstone top; a French silver one with bird design; continental silver with an engraved floral band. (Bottom row, left to right) A Middle Eastern silver thimble with a design of palms and a mosque in black – this is known as niello work; two gilt metal thimbles from Spain of a type known as Toledo, the left-hand example having the name TOLEDO on a black background on the lower band; another Middle Eastern silver niello thimble with a river scene; a continental silver example with a cherub design engraved on the lower band.

A comprehensive collection of children's and miniature thimbles in silver, enamel, ivory and brass, with 50p and 20p coins to give an idea of their size. The four thimbles at the bottom are doll's or dolls' house size.

An even smaller item is the tiny silver thimble used in the Christmas festivities and fairly common up to the outbreak of the Second World War. It was customary to put such a thimble in the mixture of the Christmas pudding, and it was supposed to bring good luck to the person in whose portion it was found. Another small thimble sometimes found is one that originates in the board game of Monopoly, made in cheap metal and having the words 'For a good girl' stamped

Spirit measures in the shape and style of thimbles, known as thimblefuls. (Left to right) Pewter with thick rolled-back rim; silver-plated; nickel with enamel souvenir plaque; green glass; pewter; another with enamel souvenir plaque; silver-plated; blackberry and cream slag glass. All these have JUST A THIMBLEFULL round the rim.

Three silver open-sided finger guards (top centre, top right and middle – the last of these three being Dutch), and three thimbles with niello decoration; the one top left is plain with a design of camels in a desert; bottom left, with a ring attached, is Russian niello, and the one bottom right has an elaborately applied silver design.

on it. Tiny silver thimbles with a loop attached to the top are charms to add to a bracelet. Even tinier items can also be found, probably intended for a dolls' house.

The opposite of these miniatures is the 'thimbleful'. These were made as measures for spirits, perhaps being intended to give the impression that only a small amount was being consumed. They were made in china, glass and metal and are exact replicas of a thimble, including the indentations, although much larger, usually about 5 cm (2 inches) in height. JUST A THIMBLEFULL is written round the edge, which is the top when it stands open end up as if holding liquid. Many china thimblefuls were made in crested souvenir wares, with the arms of towns on the sides, Goss and Arcadian being among the best-known. Some larger thimble shapes were also made that were not intended for spirit measures. Glass thimblefuls are fairly common, in clear, coloured and slag glass, the mould again being an exact copy of a thimble. Some were made by Sowerbys of Gateshead, marked with the peacock's head trademark, and others by George Davidson & Company, with their mark of a half lion emerging from a crown. Metal thimblefuls were made in pewter, copper, brass and nickel silver, and these often have a coloured souvenir shield on the side. Occasionally hallmarked

Gadget thimbles in base metals, with steel scissors. (Clockwise from left) Iles's patent, with four holes round the sides and one in the top; brass thimble with a thread-cutter attached to the side; a cupro-nickel adjustable thimble, Rosina Durham patent, possibly 1892; another type with a different style of thread-cutter; another brass thimble with thread-cutter; an elaborately decorated example with a blackberry pattern and VENTILATED ILES PATENT written round the rim.

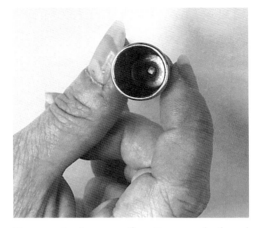

Two aspects of a thimble with a Stanhope in the top, showing views of the Forth Bridge.

silver items can be found, a version of these having been made recently.

One novelty thimble has a thread-cutter or needle-threader attached to the side, generally made in base metal. Thimble makers were frequently taking out patents for improved designs with gadgets attached, but few of these proved popular, which may explain their scarcity today.

A popular type of embroidery in the eighteenth century was tambour work. For this the fabric was stretched over a frame held in the hand, the thread then being pulled through from underneath with a very fine hook to produce a lazy daisy stitch design. A special thimble was used, consisting of a piece of rolled metal with a sloped top, in which there was a notch to hold the material and guide the hook, but these are now seldom found.

As the tourist trade developed in the Victorian period, a popular type of souvenir was a viewer or Stanhope. This was a minute collection of views of a seaside town or place of interest inserted behind a miniature magnifying glass, to be viewed against the light, the whole being no more than 3 mm ($^1/_8$ inch) in size. They were incorporated into numerous objects, including thimbles, but these must have been more novelties than practical articles and they have rarely been seen. Many viewers have lost either the pictures or the magnifying glass, or both.

Guards or shields were made to protect the finger of the hand holding the material when sewing. Some were shaped like a barrel without the ends, others like a thimble with a portion of the top removed, and others consisted of a cone-shaped unjoined rolled sheet of plain metal or plastic (sometimes coloured, or imitation tortoiseshell), which would expand to fit the finger. They were also made in plain silver, not indented, and sometimes came in a matching set with a thimble.

Some ladies used thimbles to seal their letters or parcels. In 1866 a thimble was employed to form the battery used in the first Atlantic telegraph. There are also a number of quaint customs associated with thimbles. In the old dame schools, a form of punishment was to tap a misbehaving child on the head with an iron thimble on the finger. This was known as 'thimmel-pie'. 'Thimble rigging' was another name for jiggery-pokery or sleight of hand; the trick involved placing a pea under one of three thimbles and asking the onlooker to guess and bet on the one under which the pea was to be found.

Worldwide thimbles

Interest will be added to a collection of thimbles if it includes some items from different parts of the world. Each country has its own particular styles and types, influenced by local skills and culture. The United States has a large variety of thimbles, and there were many manufacturers of silver thimbles at work there. These thimbles are frequently marked 'Sterling', with the maker's name appearing inside the top. There is also a wide choice of American advertising thimbles. A few examples are: 'Boston Mutual Life Insurance Company'; 'Hazzard shoes'; 'Holland furnaces make warm friends'; 'Hutmacher's shoe shop'; 'Jack Rose tea'; 'Olson Rug Company, Chicago'; 'Real Silk hosiery mills, Indianapolis'; and 'Singer sewing machines'. Thimbles of this type were also used to promote the election of politicians, for example 'Hoover and Curtis' or 'Whitney for Governor'. Thimble collecting is extremely popular in the United States, and there are special clubs for enthusiasts.

A distinctive type of smooth silver thimble with elaborate applied decoration, sometimes incorporating semi-precious stones, comes from Mexico. It is important to recognise these, as they were in production at least until the 1980s. Thimbles made from the striking streaked stone onyx also come from Mexico but are not now common.

Several desirable types of thimble were produced in continental Europe. Russia is well known for rare and exotic enamel as well as silver thimbles. Silver ones earlier than 1927 bear the mark '84', and those later '875', but enamel thimbles are normally now seen only as museum pieces.

Norway is associated with especially attractive thimbles of enamel on silver, with delightful colours and decoration, sometimes of Eskimo scenes. Sweden also produces silver thimbles, the mark being three crowns and a capital S. Holland is well known for Delft china thimbles in souvenir designs, mainly coloured blue and white and showing windmills and figures in national costume. From Spain come thimbles with the individual Toledo decoration of the type found on sword hilts, paper knives and other articles. The pattern is formed with imitation coloured enamel decoration on gilt metal. Many German thimbles are

A collection of American silver thimbles, showing a variety of designs and the fairly distinctive shape and style. The maker's name usually appears inside the apex.

A varied collection of thimbles from Europe and other parts of the world. Two have enamelled bands, one being Dutch and showing a Dutch scene. Three are Austrian with applied petit point embroidery, one on the top, one with a narrow band and one with the whole side decorated. One is Portuguese with a ladybird attached on the side. There are several German silver thimbles, one of which was made by Gabler and has a green stone top. One thimble is French with an engraved scene from La Fontaine's 'Fables'. Another is Indian with a heavy all-over design. The one with a cross is from Israel. There is a Mexican thimble with applied silver wire decoration and a modern tourist example of an Eskimo finger protector made of dried reindeer skin.

of silver with semi-precious hardstone tops. From France too there are silver thimbles, decorated for example with scenes from La Fontaine's *Fables*; those of mother-of-pearl have already been mentioned.

Another distinctive type, produced for the tourist trade in the Middle East, was known as *niello*; these thimbles had a black design of camels, pyramids and river scenes on a silver background.

During the Victorian period thimbles of silver were made in India, but these are now rare.

A box from China showing the stages in making cloisonné decoration on thimbles together with two separate cloisonné examples.

FROM CHINA: CLOISONNÉ PROCESS

Cloisonné, from the French "cloison", a partition or cell, is a method of enameling. This intricate technique begins with each line of the design being formed by a ribbon of copper wire, creating "cloisons" or cells. The wires are then soldered to the base. The enamel, ground to a powder and moistened with water, is then laid into the cells and fired in a kiln at 1400°F. This process of filling and firing is repeated three or four times to achieve a depth of color and shading. Finally the piece is hand ground to a smooth surface and then polished and plated.

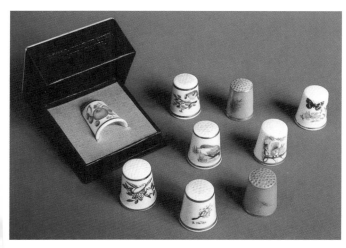

Royal Worcester porcelain thimbles. The two darker-coloured ones are cream bisque, decorated with hand-painted birds, and date from the late nineteenth to the early twentieth century. The left-hand thimble of the three at the front is decorated with a transfer print of lovebirds on a branch. The remaining white thimbles are all hand-painted, showing fruit (in the box), a blue tit and a butterfly (back, left of centre and right respectively), a kingfisher and a squirrel (centre row), and the one front centre, showing the signature, has a wren on the back and a leafy branch in front. All the white thimbles have the mark of Royal Worcester inside. The hand-painted ones are signed with the name of the artist, but the bisque ones are unmarked.

Modern thimbles

Most collections of thimbles consist mainly of items from the past, but many fairly recently made products merit inclusion in a comprehensive assemblage. Although they do not have the charm of being associated with a person from the past and cannot evoke a picture of life in days gone by, there are many craftsman-made thimbles, manufactured by traditional methods, that provide continuity with the past. These thimbles, individually painted, often signed and using, in the case of some enamels for instance, original designs of local artists, are certainly

Two boxed thimbles, enamel on brass. (Left) Made by Crummles of Poole, Dorset, commemorating the wedding of the Prince of Wales and Lady Diana Spencer in 1981. (Right) A Staffordshire design of mice on a cereal stalk. Both have gilded indented tops and gilded bottom ring.

Enamel on brass thimbles made by Crummles of Poole, Dorset, with hand-painted floral and formal designs. The two on the far right belong to a series, one thimble for each month of the year.

Four Staffordshire Enamel thimbles. (Left to right) Fleur-de-lis (shown in colour on page 13); toadstools; a floral pattern; floral design with a trellis pattern.

Four Royal Worcester porcelain thimbles, one boxed. (Left to right) A plain white design known as 'Blind Earl White', with scalloped gilded edge; 'Rosebuds' design, also with scalloped gilded edge; 'Blue Scale' pattern; and 'Royal Garden', with gilded top and bottom rings.

A collection of Spode fine bone china thimbles with the original box in which they were supplied. Most have floral transfer-printed designs, but the one at the left-hand corner of the box shows a wren at its nest, and the second thimble from the left at the bottom has ridged sides, a gilded floral top and a pale turquoise lower band with gold angel's head and wings.

Thimbles by Coalport and Mason's Ironstone (both members of the Wedgwood Group). (Left to right) Coalport 'Caughley Sprays'; Mason's Ironstone 'Monaco'; 'Christmas Tree'; and 'Violet'.

desirable and have become collectors' items. Many have interesting commemorative associations and are well designed and decorative.

Antique enamel thimbles are hard to find and have seldom survived in good condition, but modern ones have been made in their traditional home in the Midlands and in a workshop in Dorset. Their manufacture from rolled sheet copper, through the application of the designs in colourful enamels, to the final beautifully finished product is a painstaking procedure. Enamels have also been made in Scandinavia, and these too are worthy of a place in any collection.

However, most collectable thimbles were made in porcelain, by several well-known manufacturers. Royal Worcester thimbles from the past are among the most desirable collectors' items. This factory made fine hand-painted thimbles until 1985, when production ceased. After 1900 they were signed by the artists. The story of these artists holds much romance and special interest for the collector, as some artists,

Wedgwood Jasper thimbles, photographed with a quality pair of brass-handled scissors. (Back row) Dark green, with dancing lady decoration; blue, with bust of Josiah Wedgwood; dark green, with dancing lady; mauve, with bust of Josiah Wedgwood; black basalt, with gold star design. (Front row) Red, with laurel wreath; blue, with reindeer design; blue, with sheep; sage green, with bust of William Shakespeare.

A collection of Caverswall china thimbles, some hand-painted by M. Grant, others transfer-printed, including floral designs, a butterfly and other insects, a Welsh dragon and a skating scene produced for Christmas 1978.

Plastic and china transfer-printed thimbles: a small selection from a very wide range available at the modest end of the market, and one Limoges china thimble (top row, second from right), a gilded design with enamelled flowers on the top.

A collection of wooden souvenir ware containers. (Clockwise from left) A large circular Mauchline ware box with red pincushion top; a Tunbridge ware circular box with mosaic inlay top; two tartan barrels with the distinctive gilt decorative rings; a thimble-shaped box with painted flowers on the top; two similar shapes in Mauchline ware; a black painted egg with floral label and message FROM COWES; an early Tunbridge ware circular box with painted rings and rare matching thimble; and a Mauchline ware beehive shape with a transfer print of Chichester Cathedral.

Three containers in carved coquilla nut: a pear shape, an egg shape, and an acorn shape. These unscrew in the centre to reveal the thimble space.

silk, and a silver egg with a chain attached to hang on a chatelaine. A small velvet-lined trunk in pierced silver-plated metal is modern. Chatelaine eggs and box containers were made in brass, plain or with a floral decoration on the outside, lined with finely quilted blue or green silk, and neatly finished with very narrow ric-rac braid.

Ivory containers, especially boxes, are now quite rare, perhaps the most striking being a small velvet-lined basket complete with handle. Egg and acorn shapes in this material were quite common, sometimes delicately pierced or stained. Ivory also appears in an egg and eggcup design, with the cup often in ebony and the egg in ivory or vegetable ivory. Another attractive type is an ivory egg shape sometimes joined to a small cylindrical needlecase, both covered in a fine decoration of very small coloured beads. Barrels can also be found in stained ivory. Vegetable ivory is probably a more frequent material than ivory for thimble cases; there are egg and acorn shapes, together with many others, either on stands or incorporating other needlework items such as tapemeasures, waxers and pincushions.

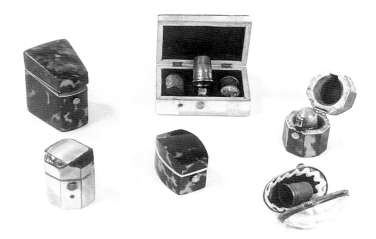

A selection of fine-quality containers. (Top, left to right) A tortoiseshell box shaped like an antique cutlery box, with a hinged lid and having space inside for a thimble and compartments separated by thin ivory leaves for packets of needles; a rectangular box covered in panels of mother-of-pearl and abalone shell, lined with blue velvet and with compartments for a matching pincushion and thread-waxer as well as the thimble; an octagonal tortoiseshell-covered box lined in rose-coloured velvet. (Bottom, left to right) A similar octagonal box covered in mother-of-pearl and abalone shell; a tortoiseshell-covered box specially shaped for a thimble; a mother-of-pearl egg with gilt metal mounts, lined in velvet.

Mother-of-pearl and tortoiseshell veneer cover a variety of small lined boxes, some shaped like an antique cutlery box with sloping lid, and others octagonal or specially shaped for a thimble, all having hinged lids that lift up. Some of the former boxes contain only a thimble, but others have a partitioned space for packets of needles. A further type is a lined rectangular box containing a thimble with matching silver pincushion and waxer. Mother-of-pearl is used for eggs with gilt metal mounts or half eggs mounted on stands or made into small carts.

Leather-covered thimble containers. The open case (upper left) and the closed one in the centre are in a fairly common rectangular shape with brass mounts, and the one top centre is a realistic trunk type with gilt banding. Two (bottom left and upper right) are thimble-shaped; these sometimes have the name of the retailing jeweller printed inside the lid on the silk lining. The three charming miniature binocular cases (far left, far right and lower right) are unusual; one has two matching thimbles, and the others have a miniature reel of thread to accompany the thimble.

A collection of well-made containers in wood (such wooden items are known as treen). (Top row, left to right) A fine early nineteenth-century rosewood urn shape on a stand, the knob-topped lid lifting off to reveal the thimble; a mahogany acorn shape on a stand; and a complete acorn on a stand in walnut. (Centre row, from left) An early Tunbridge ware bell shape in light-coloured wood with faded coloured rings; a boxwood churn shape decorated with concentric rings; and a walnut barrel. (Bottom row, left to right) An acorn shape in yew wood; an old turned rosewood thimble; and an open fruitwood container shaped like an acorn and having a rather unusual stalk continuing into the interior.

Velvet- or leather-covered brass-bound trunks were a popular shape, as were such items as a two-coloured sectioned jockey cap or a velvet-covered shell. Leather was used to cover thimble-shaped containers with hinged lids, on the inside of which one occasionally finds the name of the shop where it was sold. More unusual is a miniature binocular case containing a tiny reel of thread in addition to the thimble. Leather and velvet may also cover realistically shaped small shoes, a similar design being made in glass, the thimble resting under the

A superb pair of thimble containers, probably of continental origin, finely carved in unpolished wood, with lids featuring figures of a man and a girl.

A group of novelty animal shapes and one bird shape. (Clockwise from left) A small metal bear attached to a metal bowl with a velvet pincushion; a large continental wooden bear with a pincushion container on its back and holding a thimble between its paws; a composition material elephant holding the thimble in its back; and an Irish bog-oak owl with the thimble in its head.

A collection of metal containers. (Clockwise from top left) A rectangular brass box with stamped-out design; a decorated egg shape opening lengthways; a lined rectangular case with chain, with shaped nest for the thimble and the lid lined with quilted blue fabric, finished with a very fine ric-rac braid; a small silver egg-shaped container; an ormulu-decorated container in elaborate pattern with a ring to hang on a chatelaine; a pierced rectangular trunk shape, the hinged lid opening in the centre to reveal the red-lined interior, and with a carrying handle; a plain brass egg.

upper of the shoe. Miniature slippers, either covered in fabric or embroidered, have much charm, as also do miniature baskets with hinged lids.

One of the most frequently used materials for thimble cases is wood, including boxwood, rosewood, ebony, mahogany and fruitwoods. The shapes are varied and ingenious: egg, acorn and urn forms, walnuts and round boxes. Irish bog-oak was used decorated with Irish symbols and in upturned hat, saucepan or other shapes. From Europe came many carved wooden designs, notably bears supporting thimbles between their paws. Several types of souvenir ware were used for wooden thimble containers. Tunbridge ware, made in Tunbridge Wells, was distinctive, some being made from a number of sticks of different coloured woods glued together. From the resulting larger stick items were turned (these are known as stickware), or thin slices off the larger sticks were used as a veneer (this is known as mosaic). Many of the

A collection of novelty thimble cases. (Back row, left to right) A brass thimble topping a net-covered glass base; a green velvet shell shape, the thimble held in a clip inside; a souvenir white stone trunk with the message FROM SWANAGE; a marble souvenir obelisk, the thimble held in an opening in the front, with the message A PRESENT FROM BOURNEMOUTH. (Front row, from left) A dark red velvet-covered purse shape with brass mounts; a small wooden green-painted hat shape from Scandinavia; and a Chinese straw-work basket.

A group of thimble-shaped containers and two luxury boxed thimbles. (Clockwise from left) A dark red leather-covered thimble shape with hook fastening; a lighter red thimble shape, open to show the name of the retailing jeweller in gold lettering inside the silk-lined lid and the empty velvet thimble rest; a gold child's thimble in a red leather-covered box; a silver thimble with inset green stones in a light brown leather-covered box and the name of a Regent Street jeweller inside the lid; a cream-coloured plastic thimble-shaped case; a black leather-covered thimble-shaped case with a snap fastening.

shapes already mentioned can be found in this medium. In Scotland another popular souvenir ware used sycamore wood on to which was transferred a picture in black of a famous place or resort. Tartan ware, in which tartan patterned paper was glued on to plain wood shapes, with the name of the tartan usually printed on, also came from Scotland. Both these Scottish wares came in some of the shapes already mentioned and also in the form of bottles, beehives and saucepans. Similar items can also be found in light wood decorated with red and green ferns, seaweeds or with a design of light-coloured ferns on a dark brown background.

Plastics were used for thimble holders, making a shaped box in which the thimble was sold. This material can also be found in more elaborate sewing compendiums that incorporate needles and thread as well as the thimble, which forms a screw-on top. Some of these were made to advertise a particular product.

Thimble holders also come as metal buckets to hang on chatelaines, some plain but more often very decorative, and they are found as combination sewing sets, etuis and ladies' companions, which are small cases designed to carry sewing necessities and sometimes other tools of a personal nature.

It was because a thimble was so small and often of considerable value, not easily replaced in days when shopping was difficult, that a special container was needed to keep it safe and to hand. This fact and the variety of thimbles and their cases give the collector much scope for a fascinating hobby.

Societies

Dorset Thimble Society (for collectors of sewing tools everywhere). Membership secretaries. UNITED KINGDOM AND ELSEWHERE: Mrs Joan Mee; telephone: 01202 555427. AUSTRALIA: Mr Jack Turner, 23 Harrow Road, Somerton Park, South Australia 5044. UNITED STATES: Mrs Pat Rich, 4411 Walsh Street, Chevy Chase, Maryland, MD 20815, USA.

Needlework Tool Collectors Society of Australia Ltd, LPO Box 6025, Cromer, Victoria 3193, Australia.

Thimble Collectors International. Membership chairman: Jina Samulka, TCI Membership Chairperson, 316 Parkwood Road, Vestal, NY 13850-1262. Website: www.thimblecollectors.com

Further reading

Burn, Diane Pelham. *Identifying Steel-cored Thimbles* and Supplement. Dorset Thimble Society, 1993 and 1997.
Dreesmann, Cécile. *A Thimble Full*. Witgeverij Cambium, Utrecht, 1983.
Gaussen, Elaine. *Sewing Accessories, A Collector's Guide*. Millers, 2001.
Gowan, Susan Jean (illustrated by Betty Maloney). *Thimbles of Australia*. Kangaroo Press Pty Ltd, Australia, 1998.
Grief, Helmut. *Talks about Thimbles*. Universitätsverlag, Carinthia, Austria, for Fingerhutmuseum, Creglingen, Germany, 1984.
Groves, Sylvia. *The History of Needlework Tools and Accessories*. David & Charles, 1973.
Holmes, Edwin. *Thimbles*. Gill & Macmillan, Dublin, 1976.
Holmes, Edwin. *A History of Thimbles*. Cornwall Books, USA, 1985.
Lundquist, M. *The Book of a Thousand Thimbles*. Wallace/Homestead Company, Iowa, 1970.
Lundquist, M. *Thimble Americana*. Wallace/Homestead Company, Iowa, 1981.
Lundquist, M. *Thimble Treasury*. Wallace/Homestead Company, Iowa, 1975.
Proctor, Molly. *Needlework Tools and Accessories: A Collector's Guide*. Batsford, 1990.
Rath, Jo Anne. *Antique and Unusual Thimbles*. A. S. Barnes & Company, New Jersey, 1979.
Rogers, Gay Ann. *American Silver Thimbles*. Needlework Unlimited (PO Box 181, Claremont, CA 91711, USA), 1989.

Sewing companions, each incorporating a thimble and with sewing necessities inside. These are all twentieth-century examples. (Clockwise from top left) A cream plastic container with yellow silk tassel topped by a yellow plastic thimble; a gold-coloured metal thimble screwing on to a purple plastic container with the initials DMC (the thread manufacturers) and the company's logo; a round multi-coloured plastic container of typical Art Deco style, needing to be opened to remove the thimble; a red metal stand, with a brass thimble on the top and incorporating a tapemeasure in the base; a small multi-coloured plastic container with a dark green silk tassel, having the thimble inside; and a brass container, both the thimble and the case advertising Hudson's soap.

A group of fine containers. (Clockwise from left) A small sewing companion in white guilloche enamel, the thimble unscrewing from the base to reveal sewing implements inside; a large similarly decorated yellow enamel egg-shaped compendium, also with the sewing implements inside; a delightful china compendium, with the sewing implements inside, the thimble forming the top, and with miniature scissors attached to the decorated brass centre join; a black and red decorated white enamel egg-shaped container with a ring for hanging.

Two luxury containers. (Lower left) A rare stemmed egg shape made in horn. (Upper right) A superb two-coloured wooden stemmed egg shape (shown open) with gilt metal mounts and containing a fine quality ivory thimble with a gilt band round the base.